AP - - '17

DISCARD

EDGE
BOOKS™

Property of CLPL

EXPERIMENTAL
DRONES

by Amie Jane Leavitt

CAPSTONE PRESS
a capstone imprint

Edge Books are published by Capstone Press,
1710 Roe Crest Drive, North Mankato, Minnesota 56003
www.mycapstone.com

Copyright © 2017 by Capstone Press, a Capstone imprint. All rights reserved. No part of
this publication may be reproduced in whole or in part, or stored in a retrieval system, or
transmitted in any form or by any means, electronic, mechanical, photocopying, recording,
or otherwise, without written permission of the publisher.

Library of Congress Cataloging-in-Publication Data
Library of Congress Cataloging-in-Publication data is available on the Library of
Congress website.
ISBN: 978-1-5157-3768-1 (library binding)
ISBN: 978-1-5157-3776-6 (paperback)
ISBN: 978-1-5157-3796-4 (eBook pdf)

Editorial Credits
Carrie Sheely, editor; Steve Mead, designer; Tracey Engel, media researcher;
Katy LaVigne, production specialist

Photo Credits
Alamy: dpa picture alliance, 24–25; AP Photo: Claude Paris, Front and Back Cover; DARPA:
Joint Base Cape Cod, 10–11; Getty Images: Andreas Rentz, 18, Eric Cheng/Barcroft Media,
28–29, Ethan Miller, 26–27, John Lawson, Belhaven, 5, Ratib Al Safadi/Anadolu Agency, 23;
Lockheed Martin Aeronautics Company, 12; Newscom: BAS CZERWINSKI/EPA, 19, PIERRE
ALBOUY/REUTERS, 21; Shutterstock: Andis Rea, Design Element, Brothers Good, Cover and
Interior Design Element, DamienGeso, Design Element, katrin88888, 6, Kolonko, Design
Element, Konstantin Ustinov, Design Element, Nik Merkulov, Cover and Interior Design
Element, ohrim, 4, Pagina, Design Element, robuart, Design Element, slhy, Cover Background,
Vjom, Cover and Interior Design Element; U.S. Air Force Photo, 14–15; U.S. Navy Photo, 8–9;
Wikimedia: SpaceX Photos, 16–17

Printed and bound in China.
007890

TABLE OF CONTENTS

CHAPTER 1

PUSHING THE LIMITS OF TECHNOLOGY

A surfer parks her car at the beach. She takes a small plastic drone from the backseat. She attaches a **high-definition** video camera to the bottom. Then she straps a flight-control device that looks like a watch onto her wrist. She places the drone onto the sand, and then paddles out into the frothy ocean waves. Once she catches a good wave, she presses a button on the controller. The drone lifts off the sand and zips out toward her. It follows her as she rides the wave, catching all of the action around her. It zooms in and out to show all the angles of her ride. As her ride ends, the drone flies back to its original position on the sand. The new drone worked perfectly. Her test of the drone is finished. She will give the drone manufacturer feedback on the drone's performance. She also now has the ultimate "selfie" video.

Extreme sports athletes aren't the only people who are trying out drones. Military forces, delivery companies, and **meteorologists** are all experimenting with them. Although thousands of drones are in use, the ones in testing are pushing the limits of what drones can do.

Many drone manufacturers focus on a drone's ability to take high-quality video and photographs. Cameras can either be built-in or attached to a drone.

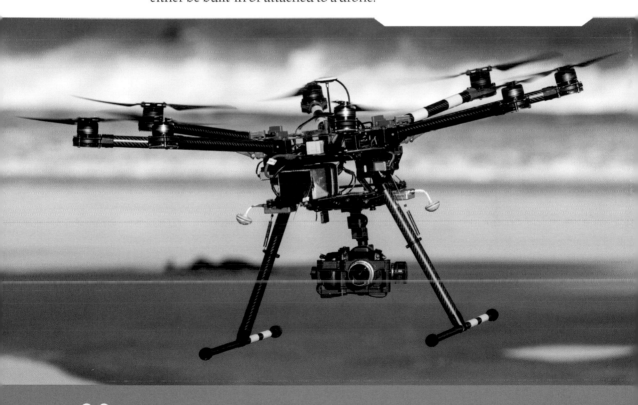

high-definition—having a high clarity of visual presentation; cameras labeled as high definition meet a certain resolution standard and other requirements

meteorologist—a person who studies and predicts the weather

CHAPTER 2

THE INS AND OUTS OF DRONES

What is a drone? Some people think of drones only as aerial vehicles. But they are much more than that. Drones that fly in the air are sometimes called unmanned aerial vehicles (UAVs). But some drones travel at sea. People usually operate drones using remote control devices. Some drones can also fly by themselves on a preset flight path. Once the flight path is set, a **Global Positioning System** (GPS) guides the drone.

Drones with four rotors are often called quadcopters.

Generally, a person is not on board a drone. But drones can carry people as passengers. The vehicle is still considered a drone if the person on board has no power to control the vehicle.

Drones come in many shapes and sizes. Military drones at sea often look like submarines. Fixed-wing UAVs look like **gliders**. **Rotor** UAVs resemble helicopters. Many rotor drones have four rotors, but some have eight or more. Some small UAVs can carry items such as books and medical supplies. Large military UAVs can carry big cameras and weapons for combat. Some of these UAVs weigh more than 4,000 pounds (1,815 kilograms) when empty.

Global Positioning System—an electronic tool used to find the location of an object; this system uses signals from satellites

glider—a lightweight aircraft that flies by floating and rising on air currents instead of by engine power

rotor—a set of rotating blades that lifts an aircraft off the ground

RECHARGING AND REFUELING

Drones have limited flight times. When their battery power or fuel runs out, they need to be recharged or refueled. Large military drones use fuel to fly. Many small drones land on a drone port on rooftops or the ground to recharge their batteries. Some researchers are looking for ways to increase flight times for drones. In 2014 a student at the Massachusetts Institute of Technology (MIT) came up with a possible way to recharge small drones using power lines. Drones would perch on a power line to recharge their batteries.

In 2016 aircraft manufacturer Boeing was granted a **patent** for a midair recharging system. The drone would have a cord called a tether. The tether could drop down and attach to a drone power station on the ground. The drone could stay in the air to be recharged instead of landing.

patent—a legal document giving someone sole rights to make or sell a product

The U.S. Navy X-47B drone refuels in flight in 2015. It was the first time an unmanned aircraft refueled while flying.

Boeing also designs sea drones. In 2016 Boeing built *Echo Voyager*. This drone submarine can dive to 11,000 feet (3,353 meters) below the water's surface. It can stay underwater for at least six months. It has a **hybrid** electric-fuel system that allows it to recharge underwater. Unlike most other sea drones, it doesn't need to return to a surface ship to recharge. After testing Boeing hopes to make these drones available for companies to buy.

hybrid—a mix of two different types; hybrid engines run on electricity and gasoline or diesel fuel

CHAPTER 3

MILITARY AND SPACE EXPERIMENTAL DRONES

The United States, Great Britain, China, Israel, and many other countries use military drones. Military drones help keep members of the armed forces out of harm's way. Many militaries partner with manufacturers to design and test drones. If testing goes well, the militaries may buy the drones. Some drone manufacturers also sell drones directly to militaries.

WEAVING AROUND OBSTACLES

In January 2016 the Defense Advanced Research Projects Agency (DARPA) completed its first flight test on a drone. The small, lightweight drone is about the size of a seagull. It carries a camera, **sonar**, and **lidar**. This equipment helps the drone fly into destroyed buildings filled with debris without crashing. It can travel 45 miles (72 kilometers) per hour while weaving in and out of obstacles. The U.S. military would like to someday use this drone to search inside unstable buildings to help keep soldiers safe.

The DARPA drone's small size would allow it to fit through windows.

sonar—a device that uses sound waves to find objects; sonar stands for sound navigation and ranging

lidar—a device that measures the distance to an object by bouncing laser light off the object and timing how long it takes the light to return; lidar stands for light detection and ranging

SR-72

Skunk Works is the advanced development program of aircraft manufacturer Lockheed Martin. Skunk Works built aircraft such as the U.S. military SR-71 Blackbird spy plane. The SR-71 was the fastest plane to have ever flown. All Skunk Works programs are important to national security, and they are secret. But future Skunk Works drones are likely to have more **stealth** technology.

The Skunk Works SR-72 Blackbird drone is planned to be finished in 2030. Lockheed plans for the drone to fly more than 4,000 miles (6,437 km) per hour. This is six times the speed of sound! Developers want it to fly undetected, take photos, and get to any location on Earth in about an hour.

an artist's drawing of the SR-72

TARANIS

Aircraft manufacturer BAE Systems built the Taranis for the British armed forces in 2010. Since then, it has completed several successful tests. The stealth drone is meant to be invisible to **radar**. The drone can travel more than 700 miles (1,127 km) per hour. The British military plans to use the test results to develop future drones and fighter planes. Some experts consider it the most advanced aircraft ever made in Great Britain.

DIVINE EAGLE

The Chinese government has recently increased its military spending. The Divine Eagle is a large **prototype** drone. It is meant to defend China's airspace and hunt enemy aircraft carriers in oceans. It has several radars to help find enemy aircraft, ships, or ground targets. The radars can detect objects on any side of the drone.

stealth—having the ability to move without being seen by radar

radar—a device that uses radio waves to track the location of objects

prototype—the first version of an invention that tests an idea to see if it will work

A TOP-SECRET SPACE PLANE

For the Boeing X-37B space drone, the skies are not the limit. The X-37B rides a rocket all the way to space. It is a joint project between NASA and the U.S. Air Force. The unmanned spacecraft is 29 feet (8.8 m) long and has a wingspan of 15 feet (4.6 m). Once in **orbit**, the X-37B flies on a preset flight path. Since its missions are top secret, little information about what the drone does is made public. Air Force officials say it is used to develop reusable spacecraft technologies and to conduct experiments.

A FUTURE HELPER FOR ASTRONAUTS

What might be the easiest way to get a snack aboard the International Space Station (ISS) someday? Send the drone! The ArachnoBeeA drone is designed to navigate inside the ISS. It is like a combination of an aerial drone and a ground robot. The drone can fly around the space station and bring items to astronauts. It also has limbs so that it can attach itself to the walls of the ISS and crawl from place to place. It has a mechanical arm that it uses to grab objects while crawling.

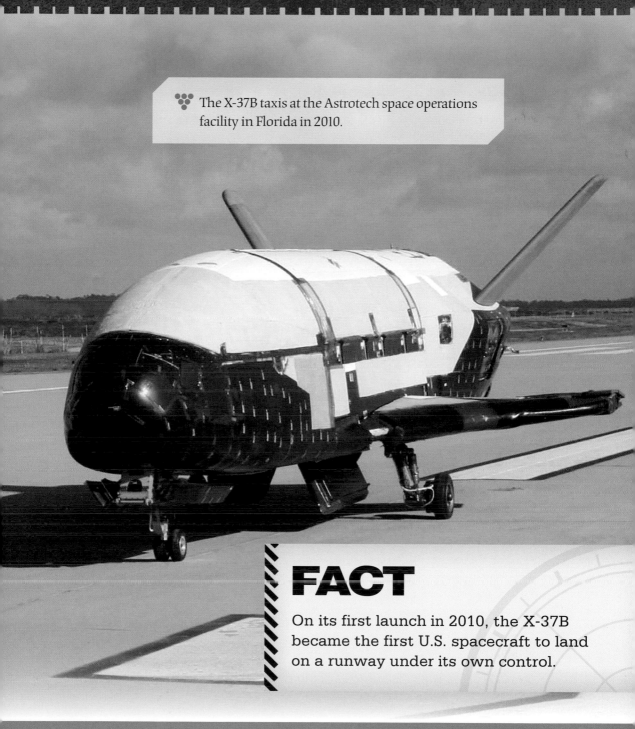

The X-37B taxis at the Astrotech space operations facility in Florida in 2010.

FACT

On its first launch in 2010, the X-37B became the first U.S. spacecraft to land on a runway under its own control.

 orbit—the path an object follows while circling another object in space

A DRONE BARGE

Space rockets require an enormous amount of energy to get into space. They have powerful engines and carry a lot of fuel. Rockets are made up of stages called boosters. Each booster is a separate part of the rocket. After the rocket is launched, the boosters separate from the rocket. The first booster separates first. Then a specific amount of time later, the second booster separates. Both boosters usually drop into the ocean. They are only sometimes retrieved by ship crews to use again.

On April 8, 2016, a Falcon 9 rocket launched from Kennedy Space Center in Cape Canaveral, Florida. But when the first booster broke off, it didn't drop into the water. Instead it landed on a drone ship that was floating in the Atlantic Ocean.

The drone ship's name is *Of Course I Still Love You*. The huge drone is a little smaller than a football field. It is 300 feet (91 m) long and 170 feet (52 m) wide. Operators can control the barge with remote control to get it in the location needed to catch the booster. Its guidance system can also be preset.

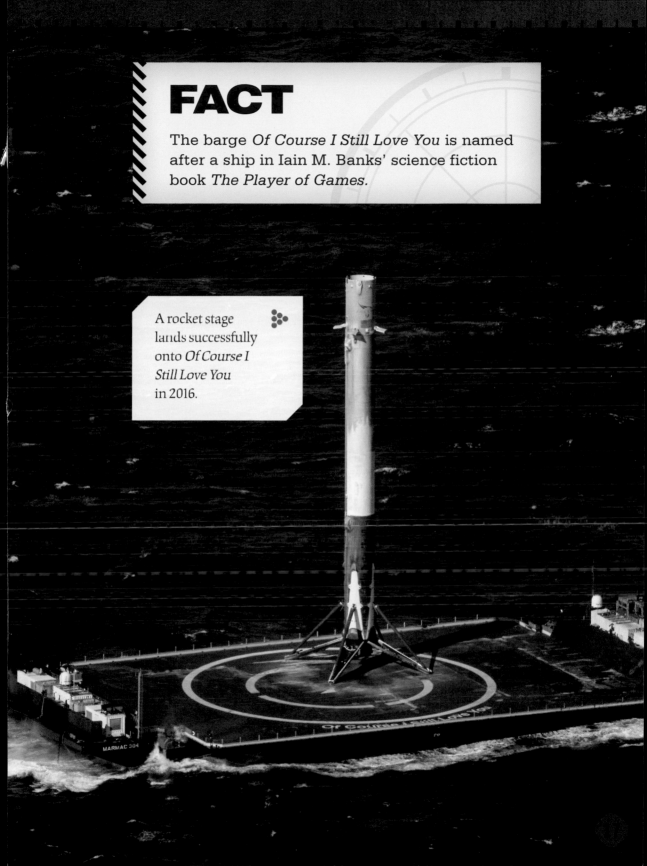

FACT

The barge *Of Course I Still Love You* is named after a ship in Iain M. Banks' science fiction book *The Player of Games*.

A rocket stage lands successfully onto *Of Course I Still Love You* in 2016.

CHAPTER 4

DELIVERY AND HUMANITARIAN EXPERIMENTAL DRONES

Imagine you're at home and hungry. You grab your computer, go online, and bring up the website of your favorite pizza place. You place your order. Twenty minutes later, your wait is over. A drone is hovering over your doorstep, and it drops a fresh pizza into your hands. Could drone delivery be common someday? Some experts think so. But there's still a lot of work that needs to be done before that can happen.

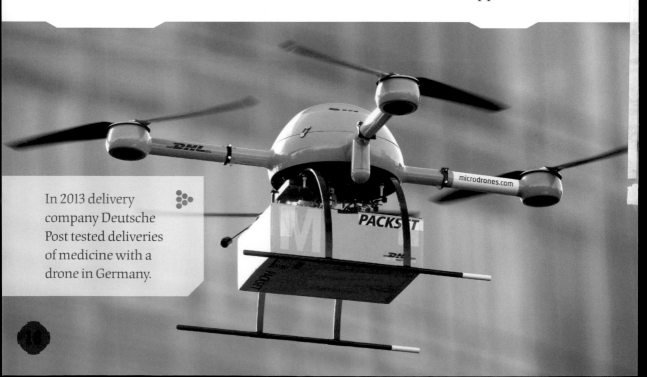

In 2013 delivery company Deutsche Post tested deliveries of medicine with a drone in Germany.

FACT

As a graduate student at Delft University of Technology in the Netherlands, Alec Momont invented a drone that could save lives. The drone was built to bring defibrillators to heart attack victims.

Around the world people have experimented with using drones for delivery service. Businesses in Great Britain have tested a variety of delivery drones. In 2013 a London restaurant used drones to deliver sushi to customers at their tables. The same year a drone delivered pizza in a test flight near London.

The German delivery company DIIL conducted test flights with delivery drones called "parcelcopters" in 2014. The drones delivered medicines and other needed goods to a remote island in the North Sea called Juist. They were some of the first European drones sent on a job outside the operator's field of vision. However, operators on the ground were able to see where the drones were going using their onboard cameras.

HUMANITARIAN DRONES

In Africa companies are testing drones to see if they can deliver food, medicine, and other important supplies to rural areas. In sub-Saharan Africa, many of the roads are not passable during the rainy season. This problem keeps many people from getting needed supplies.

A company called Matternet is working with humanitarian organization UNICEF to test drones in Malawi. In 2016 Matternet's test drone left a health clinic. It flew 6 miles (9.7 km) to a hospital. The drone carried fake blood samples. In the future Matternet hopes to carry real blood samples from newborn babies. The samples will need to be tested to see if the infants were born with **HIV**. Normally, the samples would be taken by motorcycle. This form of delivery is slow and expensive. A drone delivery system could be less costly and faster.

 HIV—a virus that causes an immune system disease called AIDS; HIV stands for human immunodeficiency virus

Matternet also hopes to someday use drones to deliver goods to people all over the world. It could let a person be both a sender and a receiver. For example, a person living in a rural village could receive goods from urban areas. Then the same person could load up the drone with homemade goods to be sold at an urban market.

A Matternet drone flies during a presentation in Switzerland in 2015.

VIEWS FROM THE SKY

The United Nations (UN) and aid organizations use drones to learn more about people's needs. Drones surveyed disaster areas after the Haiti earthquakes in 2010 and the Balkan floods of southeastern Europe in 2014. The views from the sky were especially important to help send humanitarian aid. When a disaster happens, aerial images show exactly what is going on in the area. They show where the damage is and where the most help is needed.

Aerial images from drones can also show other types of crises. In 2016 drones surveyed the size of **refugee** camps in Syria. This information helped aid organizations learn how to best help the refugees.

FACT

California company Zipline developed small fixed-wing drones. The company hopes to use the drones to deliver medical supplies in Rwanda. The drones are expected to increase the speed of delivery from weeks or months to just hours.

 refugee—a person who has to leave a place to escape war or other disasters

A rescue drone flies in Lebanon in 2015. It is designed to find people who are drowning and throw a life preserver to them.

CHAPTER 5

EXPERIMENTAL RECREATIONAL DRONES

The possibility of making life-saving medical deliveries shows the serious side of drones. But drones have a fun side too. People of all ages like playing with drones. Some people even come up with new uses for drones as they experiment.

 A drone takes photographs while shooting a movie in India in 2012.

DRONES ON STAGE

In 2014 a fleet of 15 drones flew in a concert in London's Barbican theater. The drones were costumed and lit with spotlights. They flew over the audience as an orchestra performed music on stage. The drones moved in time with the music. The producer of the event compared the coordination to that of a military operation.

The entertainment industry uses drones to make movies, stage plays, and concerts more exciting for audiences. Filmmakers like to get close-up action shots of stuntmen for their movies. To get an above-the-ground shot, directors can use helicopters. But helicopters can be very expensive. They must also stay far away from the set for the safety of the people on the ground. Drones have resolved both of these issues. They're much less expensive than helicopters and they can get very close to the action on set. Many people in the film industry feel that drones will continue to become more valuable to filmmaking.

PERSONAL FLYING MACHINE

Would you take a ride on a drone? Chinese company Ehang has invented a drone that can carry a human passenger. The Ehang 184 drone looks like a small helicopter. It has four arms. Each arm has a rotor attached to its top and bottom. The Ehang 184 is designed to carry a person weighing up to 264 pounds (120 kg).

Ehang 184 would allow people to travel short distances in the air. You would just hop on board and program in where you want to go. The drone would then transport you to your destination. Don't expect a long flight, though. It can stay in the air only about 20 minutes before needing to be recharged.

The Ehang 184 was displayed at the 2016 Consumer Electronics Show in Las Vegas, Nevada.

FACT

The "184" in the name Ehang 184 was given because the drone has one passenger, eight propellers, and four arms.

CHAPTER 6

THE FUTURE OF DRONES

The possibilities for drone use in the future are very exciting. Drone technology will continue to develop, which could lead to even more ideas. For example, today meteorologists are using aerial drones to learn more about severe weather. They fly drones into hurricanes and thunderstorms. The drones can then measure wind speed, air temperature, and other meteorological factors. In the future, drones may help scientists understand why tornadoes form, which is not fully understood today. From drones with facial recognition software to drones with **hypersonic** speed, researchers are hard at work exploring drone capabilities.

NEW RULES FOR DRONES

Major increases in drone use are expected worldwide by 2020. With this increase some people worry that drones could cause problems without more laws. Many countries have laws about drone use. In the United States, the Federal Aviation Administration (FAA) makes drone laws. Local laws may also govern drone use. Many laws focus on safety. Pilots and passengers of other aircraft need to be protected from collisions with drones. People and animals on the ground must be kept safe from crashing drones. Because many drones have cameras, personal privacy concerns also have to be considered. With laws in place, drone enthusiasts can enjoy their hobby and keep themselves and others safe.

 hypersonic—relating to a speed five or more times that of sound in air

GLOSSARY

glider (GLYE-dur)—a lightweight aircraft that flies by floating and rising on air currents instead of by engine power

Global Positioning System (GLOH-buhl puh-ZI-shuhn-ing SISS-tuhm)—an electronic tool used to find the location of an object; this system uses signals from satellites

high-definition (HI-de-fuh-NI-shuhn)—having a high clarity of visual presentation

HIV—a virus that causes an immune system disease called AIDS; HIV stands for human immunodeficiency virus

hybrid (HYE-brid)—a mix of two different types

hypersonic (hy-pur-SON-ik)—relating to a speed five or more times that of sound in air

lidar (LY-dar)—a device that measures the distance to an object by bouncing laser light off the object and timing how long it takes the light to return; lidar stands for light detection and ranging

meteorologist (mee-tee-ur-AWL-uh-jist)—a person who studies and predicts the weather

orbit (OR-bit)—the path an object follows while circling another object in space

patent (PAT-uhnt)—a legal document giving someone sole rights to make or sell a product

prototype (PROH-tuh-tipe)—the first version of an invention that tests an idea to see if it will work

radar (RAY-dar)—a device that uses radio waves to track the location of objects

refugee (ref-yuh-JEE)—a person who has to leave a place to escape war or other disasters

rotor (ROH-tur)—a set of rotating blades that lifts an aircraft off the ground

sonar (SOH-nar)—a device that uses sound waves to find objects; sonar stands for sound navigation and ranging

stealth (STELTH)—having the ability to move without being seen by radar

READ MORE

Collard, Sneed. *Technology Forces: Drones and War Machines.* New York: Rourke Educational Media, 2013.

Faust, Daniel. *Drones: Eyes in the Skies.* New York: PowerKids Press, 2016.

Marsico, Katie. *Drones.* Engineering Wonders. New York: Children's Press, 2016.

Scholastic. *Drones: From Insect Spy Drones to Bomber Drones.* New York: Scholastic, 2014.

INTERNET SITES

FactHound offers a safe, fun way to find Internet sites related to this book. All of the sites on FactHound have been researched by our staff.
Here's all you do:

Visit *www.facthound.com*

Type in this code: 9781515737681

Check out projects, games and lots more at
www.capstonekids.com

INDEX